THE MONEY SAVVY KID$ CLUB

Penny Power

Volume Four

By Susan Beacham & Lynnette Khalfani-Cox
Illustrations by Mary Jo Cadiz

Dedication

This book is dedicated to my songwriter, CFO and best friend, Michael, and my inspiration for this work, my beloved Allison and Amanda.

-Susan

Special Thanks

The authors wish to thank the following people for their brilliance and devotion

Illustrator: Mary Jo Cadiz

Editor: Cindy Richards

Poet: Michael Beacham

MoneySavvy GENERATION®
HELPING KIDS GET SMART ABOUT MONEY™

Copyright©2008 Susan Beacham and Lynnette Khalfani-Cox. All rights reserved.
Published in the United States by Money Savvy Generation, Inc.

For award-winning tools to teach kids (ages 4-16) about money choices, visit us on the web **www.msgen.com**

Publisher's Cataloging-In-Publication Data:
Beacham, Susan.
Penny power / by Susan Beacham & Lynnette Khalfani-Cox ; illustrations by Mary Jo Cadiz.
SUMMARY: Four children learn how pennies can be used to cure diseases, build schools and deliver food and medicine, and how a family's savings can help when a parent loses her job.
p. cm. – (The money savvy kids club)
ISBN 978-0-9842139-3-1
1. Money–Juvenile fiction. 2. Helping behavior in children–Juvenile fiction.
I. Khalfani-Cox, Lynnette. II. Cadiz, Mary Jo (ill.). III. Title. IV. Series.
PZ7 .B3541 Pe 2009
813–dc22
LCCN# 2009935977
2nd edition

Isaiah ran out to the playground to find his friends. He saw Sandy and Stephanie walking slowly. They looked very serious and Sandy was clearly worried. "I wonder what's wrong," Isaiah thought. Before he could ask, the bell rang and recess was over.

3

Back in class, Mrs. Berry had written something on the board. "A penny saved is a penny earned," it said. "Would anybody care to guess what this phrase means?" Mrs. Berry asked.

Sandy raised her hand. "I've heard my mom say that," Sandy said. "But I don't see what the big deal is. What can you do with one penny?"

A penny saved is a penny earned.

"I am glad you asked, Sandy," Mrs. Berry said as she pointed to three piles of pennies on her desk. The first pile contained just one shiny penny, the next had 10 and the last had 100 pennies. "Each of these piles will teach us a lesson about money," Mrs. Berry said.

"The smallest one will teach us how to become a millionaire." The students gasped. They thought Mrs. Berry must have made a mistake.

"The pile with 10 pennies will teach us how to help cure a very bad disease," Mrs. Berry continued. Again, the class couldn't believe what she was saying.

"And the pile with 100 pennies will teach us how to help build schools and deliver food and medicine to hundreds of needy children," Mrs. Berry said. Now they thought Mrs. Berry was completely crazy.

Dennis raised his hand and asked, "But, Mrs. Berry, how could a few pennies do all of that?"

"That's what I want each of you to figure out," Mrs. Berry told the class. "This weekend, I want all of you to solve the mystery of how one penny can turn someone into a millionaire, how 10 pennies can cure a disease and how 100 pennies can help hundreds of children."

"Boy, is this going to be a long weekend," Stephanie mumbled unhappily.

It was 4:00 p.m. Friday, time for the weekly meeting of The Money Savvy Kids Club. The friends had started the club to learn about money and how to handle the occasional money challenge, like the one Mrs. Berry had given them. "This meeting of The Money Savvy Kids Club is called to order," Isaiah announced, looking at the glum faces of his three best friends. "Cheer up, guys. This is our thing – we know money. We can solve these penny mysteries."

Dennis turned to Sandy. "Sandy, maybe your mom can help. She's an accountant, right? So she knows a lot about money."

"Sandy, are you listening?" Dennis asked.

"Sorry, Dennis, I was thinking about last night when I heard my mom and dad talking. Mom said her office is closing and she is being laid off starting this week."

"Laid off?" asked Isaiah. "What does that mean?"

Dennis answered first. "My mom was laid off last year. It's when you lose your job."

"Yeah. And when you are laid off, you don't make any money," Sandy said.

Now Isaiah understood why Sandy had looked worried out on the playground. "Have you asked your mom and dad about what you heard?" Isaiah asked.

"No, I'm afraid to ask them," she said.

Isaiah walked over, sat next to Sandy and said gently, "I know you're afraid, Sandy, but I think you need to gather some more facts. You may not have the whole story."

"And everything might be OK, Sandy," Dennis said. "When my mom lost her job last year, she ended up getting a job she liked even better and now she's doing great."

"I know she'll find another job," whispered Sandy, "but how will we pay our bills right now?"

"Even though your mom lost this job, she is still an accountant," Dennis said. "Accountants help other people manage their money and pay their taxes. I bet your parents already have a plan for paying the bills until your mom gets a new job."

Sandy nodded her head 'yes' in agreement with Dennis. "You know, I think you may be right, Dennis," she said. "I bet they do have a plan. I just need to figure out how to ask them about it."

"I have an idea," Stephanie said. "Why don't you ask your mom for help on our one penny mystery? Ask her how she thinks one penny can make you a millionaire. Maybe after you talk about that, you can ask her about her plan for paying the bills until she gets a job."

"That's a good start – on Sandy's problem and the one penny mystery," Isaiah said. "But we have two more piles of pennies. Any ideas about them?"

"Dennis and I can go to the library to see if we can find anything about the 10 pennies," Stephanie said.

"Great," Isaiah said. "That leaves the 100 penny mystery for me."

The friends agreed to meet again on Saturday afternoon to share what they had learned. While the other three talked more about their plans, Isaiah opened his notebook and wrote something down.

13

That night, while Sandy and her mom were doing the dishes, Sandy told her about their penny mystery. "Mrs. Berry said 'a penny saved is a penny earned' but none of us understood how that could help us become a millionaire," Sandy said.

"I seem to remember that quote has something to do with Ben Franklin," Mrs. Savingston said.

"Do you mean the Ben Franklin who studied electricity with a kite that was struck by lightning?" Sandy asked.

"Same guy," her mom said.

Sandy couldn't imagine what a kite and electricity had to do with pennies and millionaires. Instead, she gathered her courage and blurted out, "Hey, Mom, I heard you and Dad talking last night. If you don't have a job, are we going to be able to pay the bills?"

Sandy's mom dried her hands and took Sandy's hand and led her to the table. "Sandy, we are going to be just fine," she said. "When I was working, your dad and I took a part of every paycheck I earned and we 'paid ourselves first.'"

"What do you mean?" Sandy asked.

"Every time I got paid, the first thing we did was take some money and put it into a savings account. The money in that account was able to grow," she said.

"Grow?" asked a wide-eyed Sandy.

"Well, not literally grow, Sandy, but the money in our savings account earned *interest*," she said. "That's the money the bank pays you for keeping your savings there."

Sandy still looked confused.

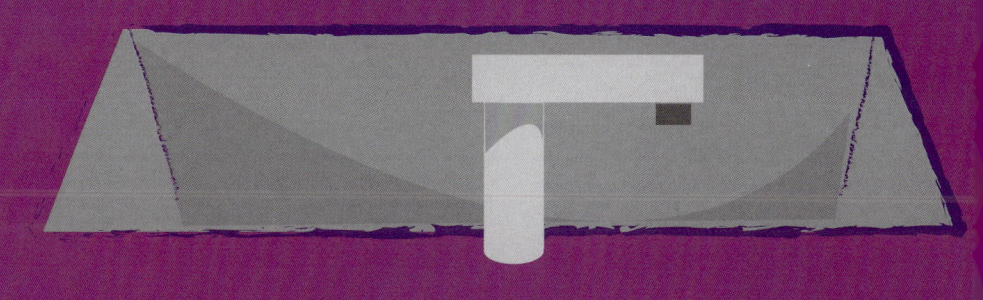

"Let me try this another way," her mom said. "Let's say I have $100 in the bank and the bank agrees to pay me 10 percent interest on the money. After the bank pays me the $10 interest it owes me, I have $110 in my savings account, right?"

Sandy nodded her head 'yes'.

"The next time I get paid interest, I will get interest on $110. So the bank will pay me $11 – 10 percent interest on $110. Now I have $121 in my savings account, even though I only deposited $100," she said.

"Oh, you mean your money grows because of compound interest," Sandy said.

Her mom was impressed. "How do you know about compound interest?"

"Mrs. Berry just taught us about compound savings in math class. Let me get my notes." Sandy dried her hands and ran to get her back pack. "Yep, here it is right here Mom, in last week's notes. We learned that if you put just $4 a day, every day in a savings account that pays you 5 percent interest, your savings would be worth $427,025 when you're 67 years old. Only $80,352 is from the daily $4 deposits. The other $346,673 is the interest."

"Maybe I should be getting advice from you from now on," Mrs. Savingston said with a laugh. "I guess old Ben Franklin was right, a penny saved **is** a penny earned."

"Thanks, Mom, I think we just solved my penny mystery," Sandy said as she jumped up to give her a hug.

Now it was her mom's turn to look confused.

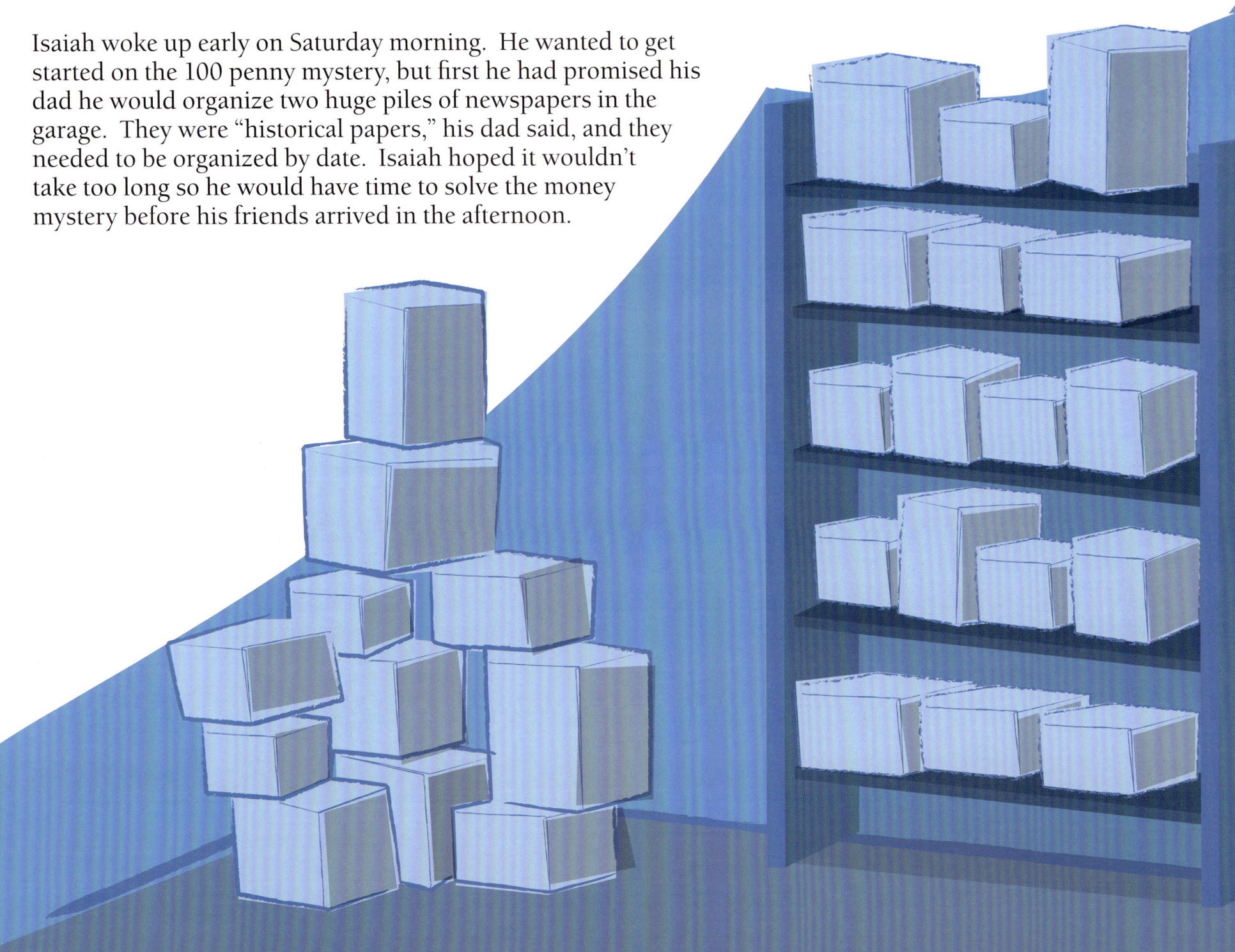

Isaiah woke up early on Saturday morning. He wanted to get started on the 100 penny mystery, but first he had promised his dad he would organize two huge piles of newspapers in the garage. They were "historical papers," his dad said, and they needed to be organized by date. Isaiah hoped it wouldn't take too long so he would have time to solve the money mystery before his friends arrived in the afternoon.

As Isaiah sorted through the papers, he stumbled upon one that told an amazing story. On October 11, 2001, President George W. Bush had asked all American children to send $1 to the White House to help poor children in Afghanistan. In just three weeks, the children had sent in over $1 million to help build schools and buy school supplies and medicine for Afghan children.

Isaiah stopped reading and reached for his notebook and pencil to take some notes.

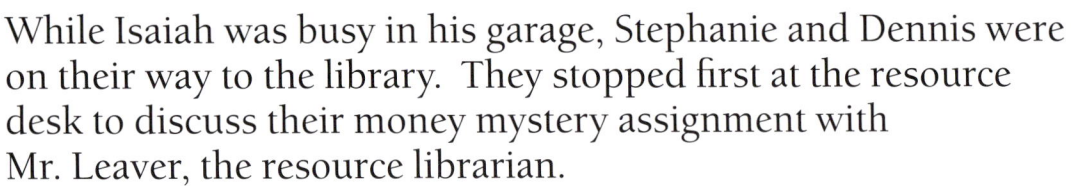

While Isaiah was busy in his garage, Stephanie and Dennis were on their way to the library. They stopped first at the resource desk to discuss their money mystery assignment with Mr. Leaver, the resource librarian.

"I seem to remember something about 10 pennies and President Franklin Roosevelt," said Mr. Leaver, stroking his chin. "Why don't you look for information on President Roosevelt?" It didn't take long for Dennis and Stephanie to discover how 10 pennies had helped cure a horrible disease.

Quiet please!

Armed with their answer, Stephanie and Dennis raced back to Isaiah's house. Sandy was already there. "What are you doing with all these papers?" Sandy asked Isaiah.

"I promised my dad I would organize these papers for him but I got distracted when I found this," Isaiah said.

"What is it?" Stephanie asked.

He told them about President Bush's request that all kids in America send $1 to the White House to help children in Afghanistan and how much they sent.

"I remember that!" Sandy said. "I cleaned the boards in Mrs. Berry's classroom that week and she paid me $1 so I could send it to the White House."

"I think we just solved our 100 penny mystery," Isaiah said. "100 pennies equals…"

"$1!" everyone shouted at once.

"And $1 from a million children equals…"

"$1 million!" the four members of The Money Savvy Kids Club shouted.

"And I solved the one penny mystery," Sandy said.

"Really? How?" Isaiah asked.

"Remember when Mrs. Berry taught us about compound interest?" she asked. Her friends all nodded their heads 'yes'. "That's how my parents are going to pay the bills until my mom finds another job. My mom and dad have been saving their money and keeping it in the bank," Sandy said.
"Dennis, are you listening to me?"

"What?!" Dennis said. "No, I'm sorry, Sandy. I was reading this article about Miss Osceola McCarty."

"Who's that?" asked Stephanie.

"She's a lady who worked washing and ironing other people's clothes for over 75 years. At first, she charged $1.50 to $2 a bundle. Later she charged about $10. She had to quit school in the sixth grade to take care of her mom and grandmother and aunt."

"That sounds like a lot of hard work," Isaiah said.

"It was," Dennis said, "but it says here it was work she was happy to do."

"Who could be happy to do hard work?" mumbled Stephanie.

Dennis ignored her and kept reading. "It says Miss McCarty opened a savings account when she was in elementary school. She kept working and saving money until one day she had a lot of money in her savings account."

"Did she buy a really nice house?" Stephanie asked.

"No," Dennis said. "She saved her money and never took any of it out of the bank. Before she died, she gave some to her church and some to her family and $150,000 to the University of Southern Mississippi to help kids like her who might not be able to afford college."

"She gave it all away?" Stephanie said, sounding shocked.

"It says here it was the biggest gift ever given to Southern Mississippi by an African American," Dennis said.

Isaiah sat down on the pile of papers and scribbled something in his notebook.

"OK, we have figured out the one penny mystery and the 100 penny mystery. What about the power of 10 pennies?" Isaiah asked.

Stephanie waved a computer printout. "Dennis and I found the answer by researching the life of President Franklin Roosevelt," she said.

Dennis went on to explain that President Roosevelt was a victim of a virus called polio. In 1938, thousands of children were getting sick with polio, and he wanted to find a cure. President Roosevelt felt that people could solve any problem if they worked together. He asked Americans to send their dimes to the White House to help pay for research to create a polio vaccine.

"People sent in so many dimes that the White House was overwhelmed," Stephanie said. "The money was used to start the March of Dimes, a charity that still funds research to stop birth defects. Those first dimes were used to help Dr. Jonas Salk create the polio vaccine all children get today."

Sandy was amazed. "Wow! All that with just 10 pennies."

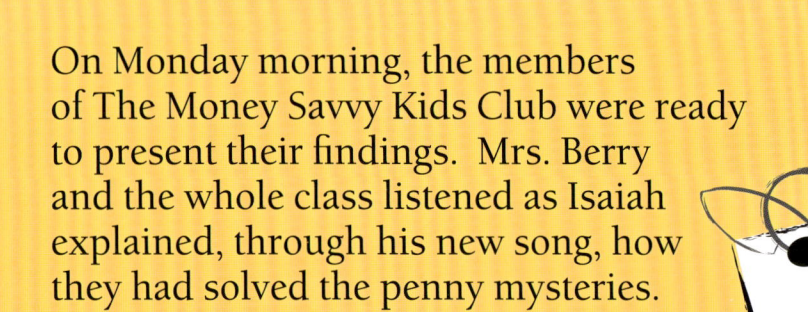

On Monday morning, the members of The Money Savvy Kids Club were ready to present their findings. Mrs. Berry and the whole class listened as Isaiah explained, through his new song, how they had solved the penny mysteries.

It's really quite funny,
This thing called money.

A very important lesson
That you must learn
Is that a penny saved
Is a penny earned.

When you save a little
Every day
Your savings can grow
In a phenomenal way.

Save just four dollars a day
And through the magic of compounding
You'll end up with half a million
Give or take, with rounding.

Save a little more daily
Just eight dollars, I swear
And by the time you retire
You'll be a millionaire.

As a nation of savers
We can cure a disease
Those extra dimes we won't miss
Can do it with ease.

And in case of emergency
There's no need to dismay
There's no need to pay the bills with the money
That you've put away.

Mrs. Berry said the class had just earned a field trip for their hard work.

Sandy raised her hand. "I think we should go to the ABC Bank."

"Why is that?" asked Mrs. Berry.

"Now that we know a penny saved is a penny earned, it might be fun to open a savings account and start practicing what we have learned," Sandy said.

"After all," Stephanie added, "if we want to be money savvy, we need to start right now."